Diving for Treasures

Also by Ralph Metzner

Allies for Awakening (2015)
The Toad and the Jaguar (2013)
Eye of the Seeress – Voice of the Poet (2011) German/English poem translations
Birth of a Psychedelic Culture (2010) with Ram Dass & Gary Bravo
Sacred Vine of Spirits – Ayahuasca (ed. 2006)
Sacred Mushroom of Visions – Teonanácatl (ed. 2005)
Green Psychology (1999)
The Unfolding Self (1998)
The Well of Remembrance (1994)
Through the Gateway of the Heart (ed. 1985)
Know Your Type (1979)
Maps of Consciousness (1971)
The Ecstatic Adventure (ed. 1968)
The Psychedelic Experience (1964) with Timothy Leary & Richard Alpert

CDs
Spirit Soundings (2012) Poems, with music by Kit Walker
Bardo Blues (2005) Songs with Piano

Diving for Treasures

Poems

&

Epilogs

Ralph Metzner

Four Trees Press
2015

[paperback]
ISBN 13: 978-1-954925-13-7

[e-book / Kindle]
ISBN 13: 978-1-954925-02-1

[e-book / EPUB]
ISBN 13: 978-1-954925-03-8

Library of Congress Control Number: 2015934960

Cover Photo
Ralph Metzner

Layout and Design
Cynthia Smith

FOUR TREES PRESS
PO Box 692
El Verano, CA 95433
www.FourTreesPress.com

Contents

Shaman's Song

During the first half of my life,
I wove the threads and textures
of my experience
into a multi-colored tapestry,
dancing with images
of beauty and terror.

Now in the ending half of my journey,
this has become a magical carpet,
on which I shall sail
high over the mountains
into the radiant worlds
of boundless mystery.

Four Haiku on the Transmutation of the Elements

Air currents of mind
swiftly soaring and flying,
back to beginning.

Waves of compassion
this healing flow of feeling,
joy ever present.

Fiery radiant heat
illumined cave of caring,
tending to the flame.

Sensing hand reaches
skin contacting earth and rock
as it is, just so.

Sky of Love

It is the fulfillment of an ancient dream,
  unknown before, this love of ours.
Out of the darkness, hearts trembling with fear,
  ecstasy comes. The light shines clear,
now that we're falling free, hands linked above
  through the immeasurable sky of love.

Ancestral Tree

From tangled roots of past conditions,
genes twisting strands,
loops and turns of prior forms and stories,
unfolding...enfolding...
in the ecstasy of conception,
when Spirit ignited the fusion
of seed and egg –
I entered.

Nourished in the womb
of Sea-Earth-Mother,
cells rushed headlong to divide and grow,
made tissues, embryonic organs, fetal limbs.
Emerging then from Earth-Sea-Mother
to meet and breathe with Light-Air-Father,
at the dying –
of my birth.

Trunk now rising up,
with each year's coiling of the solar round,
earth-juice rising,
sky-fire coursing down,
building and re-building form,
in-forming Self –
joyful embodiment.

Branches press out,
make bridges for Self,
to reach and to touch,
bend with the wind,
sensing Nature's intricate ways.
Gently putting out fruit and seed,
fruits that nourish,
seeds that grow.

Willingly, gladly, releasing
sparkling leaves of light.
With endless longing
we unfold antennae for Spirit.
Trembling as they register
God's breath –
our life.

The Old Basque Seer

The crown of my head tingled
    every time I was near him.
This was the energy of visions coming through,
    I was told.

One felt transparent to the unwavering gaze
    of his gentle eyes, under thick black eyebrows.
Wisps of white hair clung to his skull,
    long like those of the Maya and ancient Egyptians.

He would sit motionless,
    eyes glancing at trees, children, birds,
    dancing with inner visions:
Dreams perhaps, meetings with
    relatives in other worlds,
    consorting with spirits,
    practicing the strong eye.

In memory of Salvador Arrien

Nearly paralyzed, his face showed no trace of pain,
     even as he dragged his massive frame,
     breathing hard,
     laborious, yet no hint of helplessness.
He seemed to be studying with detached curiosity
     the progressive decay of his body –
     impeccable scientist.

Sheep-herder, vision-maker for his community,
     always generous, kind and direct in his speech.
Most often, in the last years,
     his only response to a question
     would be an eyebrow jumping up,
     as if a cricket lived in it.

His face expressing child-like innocence and delight,
     no judgment and unswerving focus –
     compassionate master seer.

A Tree Has Been Cut Down

The giant trees stand in a circle,
silently communing with the one
who lies felled on the forest floor.

"One of us has been cut down."
The form but not the Being within the form.

Your freedom is our loss, beloved friend.
No longer do you walk with us on the Earth path,
your precious human form destroyed.

But you, Immortal Soul, dancing freely now,
moving as lightning, or wind, or winged spirit,
communing with us in our earth-body sleep.

Farewell, dear friend, as you depart
to that unknown country.
And we can remember
the Oneness of all Being.

In memory of Phyllis Jackson, colleague and friend, who was murdered in 2003
in San Francisco, by her demented step-son.

Palenque

We sit in silence on the steps
of the House of Our True Lord,
in the soothing silvery light
of the full Moon, embraced by
the goddess Ix'chel.

And the spirits of the noble
Maya lords and ladies,
halach uinic, zac uinic,
the "true humans," the "bright ones,"
who left this place a thousand years ago,
graced our presence
in a moment of unspeakable beauty,
and flowered again
in our dreams.

Gratitude to my friend Christian Rätsch, German anthropologist and Mayanist,
who was our guide on a tour of Maya sites in Yucatan, in the late 1980s.

Dachau

I stood in the place of small white pebbles and wept.
Silently we regard the memorial. A sign says –
"Let us always remember the dignity of man."

Huge photos, facts and figures testify
to the arrogant scorn of "man the knower"
toward those of his own kind.

We who are the descendants of Adam and Eve,
were instructed to know and to name the creations
and to honor the Creator
with our inspired words and images
and the deeds of our hearts and our hands.

Oppression, torture, murder, violence –
these were not to be practiced,
but recognized and remembered
in ourselves and in others.

This is why I wept in Dachau,
in this sacred, sun-drenched place
with small white pebbles –
where Love sacrificed herself to Death.

The Grieving Heart of the World Mother

O Mother, your children have so much sorrow.
Millions of arms reach out to you:

> the woman grieving for her dying child,
>
> the lover longing for his beloved lost,
>
> the bitter pain of those stung by injustice,
>
> the cold aching of unwanted children,
>
> the silent sorrow of neglected elders,
>
> the moaning of the sick and tortured.

All these cry out to you for solace and for relief
> from bewilderment and despair.

This poem, and the previous one, were written in the 1980s, when I was traveling in Southern Germany, visiting concentration camps and shrines of the Black Madonna.

And there are also those who
    have closed off their human heart,
    hurting and killing others
    to deaden their own inner terror –
    these too are screaming in anguish.

And you hear them, O Mother, like the others,
    and with Infinite Compassion
    you embrace them all in your grieving heart,
    sharing patiently your boundless love and support,
    and your luminous knowing of the Immutable Law.

Two Short Love Poems

I

When I am inside of you
You are the flower
I am the bee.

When you are inside of me
You are the wood nymph
I am the tree.

II

As we merge
with each other
I want to look
into your eyes, shining
with a wild sweetness.
I sink through them,
falling
tasting
deep violet pool
of desire
fulfillment.

I Am Here

I am here because the sea is blue and in love with the sky.

I am here because I want to listen to the ringing of crystal.

I am here because the world is too vast to contain
    in the depth of the night.

I am here because the light of nature has brought me
    to the edge of nowhere.

I am here because the door in the back of my heart
    opens to the garden of laughter.

The Reason I Could Not Speak Before

I was overwhelmed,

by too great a cresting wave of feeling

for the three-fold goddess in my family.

For you my lover, wife and friend,

lioness mother with flowing breast,

fragrant, smiling, silken limbs,

companion of journeys in dreams and times.

And you, daughter of five breathing days,

you of the rose-petal cheeks, the softness glowing,

swiftly changing joy, surprise and wonder –

infant goddess, sparkling flower.

My daughter was born in California on the same day that my mother died in London. This poem was inspired in a moment of speechlessness at this encounter with the Goddess in three forms.

And you, mother of all my days,
peaceful now that all is fulfilled.
Legs walk no more, mind comprehends no more.
Ah – the letting go into the white stillness.

And you, great Living Stream of Deaths and Births,
Great Knowledge Tree of Earth,
Great Mother of boundless, curving space,
Great Father of all-embracing light.

Joyful the song.
Blissful the silence.

Life Cycle Medicine Wheel

The child in me reacts –
    with joy and sadness, affection and fear,
    to the dazzling presentations of the world.
Youthful spontaneity, sparked by curiosity,
    protected by the angels of innocence.

The man in me responds –
    arms of compassion reaching out,
    feet of adventure walking forth.
Mind's creativity shapes the sound,
    delights in the voice and the dance of the god.

The woman in me receives –
    the flowers of meaning, the fruits of knowing,
    gathered by the eyes, the ears and the senses.
Moist warm the cauldron of the body,
    bringing forth sweet gifts of the love of the goddess.

This and the following five poems are recorded on my CD Spirit Soundings, with music by Kit Walker and friends.

The old one in me reflects –
　on the long journey taken and the roads not chosen,
　the allies and enemies,
　the parents and children.
The places and stories
　of birthing and dying.

　No regret.
　No blame.
　No struggle.
　No boundary.

Diving for Treasures

Here, in the cave of the heart, slowly,
the soul's eye descends to the depths.

Crystal diving sphere,
omnidirectional lens,
scanning organic inner realms,
cellular mother ocean bed,
molecular web and net,
interconnected to infinity,
pulsing vibrational streams.

Light! Darkness!
Light!

You are seeking the pearls
of golden energy-essence,
guarded by the dragon,
dwelling in the labyrinth of memory.
That dragon's name is
pain-fear-threat-scream.

This poem was inspired by an experience with the entheogenic snuff 5-meo-dmt, which was also code-named Jaguar in underground circles. It is described in my book The Toad and the Jaguar. I originally gave the poem two sub-titles: one was solutio, a term from the alchemical healing tradition referring to the dissolving of rigid defensive armoring structures in the body-heart-mind complex. The other sub-title was absorption, a term from the hypnotherapy tradition referring to a state of being totally absorbed, with all senses, in a deep healing trance.

Speak softly to that dragon,
Or sing to him soothingly, like Orpheus.
Then, you may take the precious pearls
from his frightful, flaming jaws.

You must thank that dragon,
for guarding them so well.

Or, you may find the sunken ship,
forgotten, with caskets of treasures,
gifts from the angels of childhood.

Or, you may find them buried,
under the sands of time and of sleep.

The diver gathers these precious jewels,
these stones of wisdom,
these sparkling elemental essences,
and brings them to surface awareness,
into the light-filled cave of your heart.

From there to the soles of the feet,
for the understanding of that which is,
and to the crown of the head,
for the visions of what may be.

Omens for Our Planetary Future

For one hundred years now
wise teachers and elders have urged:
>"We must bring together the spirituality of the East,
>>with the energy and material mastery of the West."

The Tibetan Oracle said:
>"When the iron horse flies,
>>the *dharma* will come to the Land of the Red Man."

This prophecy has come to pass.

And behold, a new vision arises, for a new century:
>"The people of the Northern nations
>>will relate with respect and justice,
>>not violence and greed,
>>to the uncounted millions of the Southern countries,
>>and the land, the forests and the riches of the earth."

The prophet seers of the Incas say:
>"The Condor of the South and the Eagle of the North
>>will fly together, in freedom."

The visionary serpent vine says:
   "The Bear and the Wolf of the North,
      the Jaguar and the Lion of the South
      will track together and hunt together,
      for vibrant life and healing knowledge."

The great Serpent of the Amazon forest,
the wise Turtle of the California desert,
      will share their ancient secrets again –
      with humans humble enough to want to learn –

      to live in balance with one another,
      and with the Earth,
      embracing and nourishing her children,
      Great Goddess Mother of All the Living.

Ayahuasca Serpent Vision

I pray to the serpent vine of visions:
    Help me heal the ancient wounds.

Slowly, the glittering snakes glide and slide,
insinuating intimately into my deepest roots.

I'm inside the Serpent Mother now,
coiling, writhing, turning, squirming,
our bodies merged – one skin, one spine.

The space within expands to spaciousness.
Our little band of travelers on the spirit boat,
in the house, on the river, in the snake,
sailing serenely along the darkening stream.

The Great Serpent's body expands once more,
encompassing now the River of Time,
the barque of human civilizations.

Whole villages and towns I see, temples and palaces,
pyramids and towers, kingdoms and nations –
    Egypt, Rome, India, America,
carried by the currents of collective fate,
    through the millennia.
One great Stream, one great Snake.

Now – continents and oceans, cloud mountains I see,
    vast deserts, rain forests, river deltas –
shimmering body of Diamond Rainbow Serpent,
Mother of All Organic Life on Earth.

And now – the Earth with her companion worlds,
    Moon, Venus, Mercury and Mars –
spinning and whirling, stately serpentine orbits,
around Primordial Mother-Father Sun.

The barque of hundreds of millions of years sails on,
    Great Cosmic Star Sun Serpent –
wheeling majestically around the Milky Way,
Galactic Center, Dark Source of All Radiance.

Remembering Your Dying
A Thought Experiment

What if this day, today, were the day of your dying?

If you remind yourself of the certainty of the fact
of its arrival – some day –
that will help you envision your mind state
on that particular last day of your life.

You may then ask yourself –
your Wise Self –
what this day will be like for you.

What will be your mood?
Who will be there with you?
With whom have you been sharing your life?
Will you put your attention to remembering
the choices you made,
the roads chosen and those not chosen,
and the consequences of those choices?

And will you let your awareness expand
beyond the veils of non-knowing
into the Hereafter?

Perhaps when you do this,
you will find yourself remembering
previous dyings –
in other lifetimes –
and smile.

Warrior's Homecoming

Welcome home, noble warriors,
     all you who have fought and struggled for so long.
Lay down your swords, your guns –
     you will not need these weapons here,
in the Great Hall of Peace.

Take off your garments stained with blood
     and wipe the war-paint off your face.
Let the healers bind your wounds,
     and clothe yourself in fresh, clean linen.
Then come – to the Great Hall of Peace.

We will want to hear your stories –
     of fearsome monsters, the madness of destruction,
     the tales of treachery and sacrifice,
     the bravery of true friends.
So welcome – to the Great Hall of Peace.

The warriors and the workers
     can rest now in friendship,
     and be at home
     with their families and the children,
     with all of us
     in the place of belonging –
in the Great Hall of Peace.

The Song of the Pearl
A Gnostic Hymn of the Soul

When I was a little child
living in my kingdom, in my father's house,
happy in the beauty and the riches
of my family that nurtured me,
my parents gave me provisions
and sent me forth from our home in the East.

My Father of Truth and
my Mother of Wisdom,
they made a bundle for me,
from their treasure house,
to carry with me on my journey.
It had gold and silver from the
House of the Highest One,
ruby and sapphire and emerald,
and indestructible diamond.

I left behind my robe of glory,
and my cloak of royal purple.

They made a covenant with me
and wrote it in my heart so I would not forget:
"When you go down into the material world
and bring back the One Pearl,
which lies in the center of the sea,
and is guarded by the fierce dragon –
you will have again your robe of glory
and the royal cloak – and with your Twin,
you will inherit the kingdom."

I left the East and went down,
with my two royal envoys,
since the way was dangerous and harsh
and I was very young to walk alone.

When I came down into the dense realms,
my companions left me,
and I went to the place of the serpent
and settled in close by his dwelling,
waiting for him to sleep,
so I could take that pearl from him.

Since I was all alone,
I was a stranger to others,
so I put on clothes like theirs, lest
they suspect me as an outsider.
When they learned
I was not from their country,
they gave me of their food and drink.

Through the heaviness of their food and their drink,
I fell into a deep trance, and then
I forgot I was a child of Royal Parents
and I forgot about the precious pearl
for which my parents had sent me.

And when all these things happened,
my Parents knew and they grieved for me.

They wove a plan on my behalf,
so I would not be lost in the material world.
They wrote me a letter and all the noble relatives
signed it also: "From your Father and Mother,
the King and the Queen, and your twin,
to our child who is in the world – greetings!

Awake and arise from your sleep
and hear these words of our letter.
Remember that you are a child of Royal Parents
and see the slavery of your life.
Remember the precious pearl,
for which you went down into the world!

Remember your robe of glory
and your cloak of royal purple,
which you may one day wear again,
when your name is written in the Book of Life,
and you and your twin shall
inherit the kingdom."

The letter was sealed against evil spirits
by my father's right hand.

And serving as messenger
to deliver the letter,
was an eagle, King of all Winged Beings.
It flew and alighted beside me,
and became speech.

At its voice and the sound of its rustling,
I awoke and rose from my sleep trance.

I took the letter and kissed it,
broke the seal and read it.
And the words written in the letter
were the same that were written in my heart.

I remembered I was the Child of Kings,
and my free soul longed for its own kind.
I remembered the Pearl
for which I had come down into the world.

I began to sing and to enchant
that terrible fierce serpent.
I charmed him to sleep,
by naming the name of my Royal Father
and Mother and my twin also.
Then I grasped the Pearl and
I turned to take it back home.

I took off the filthy and impure garments
I had worn and left them lying in the field,
as I directed my way back
into the light of our home in the East.

On my way, the letter that had awakened me
was lying on the road,
and as it had awakened me with its voice,
now it guided me with its light.
Its voice soothed my fear
and its love urged me on.

My robe of glory that I had taken off
and the royal cloak over it,
had been sent by my parents
and was being kept safely
in the hands of trusted friends.

I had forgotten the robe's splendor,
for as a child I had left it
in my Father's House.
And as I gazed on it,
the garment seemed to be a mirror,
in which I saw my whole self, but also
part of myself – we were two entities
yet in one form.

This robe of many colors
was embroidered with gold and silver threads,
with rubies and sapphires and emeralds,
its seams fastened with diamonds.
I saw the robe quiver all over
with the movements of *gnosis*,
and it started to speak,
as it moved towards me,
murmuring its song:

"We were brought up together
and grew together,
in the house of the Father-Mother."

With regal movements
It was coming towards me,
urging me to take it,
and love urged me to receive it –
so I stretched forth and received it.
I put on the beautiful robe of many colors,
all around me.

And so I clothed myself and ascended
To the gate of salutation and adoration.
I bowed my head and adored
the majesty of the Mother-Father.
They received me and rejoiced in me,
And I was with them in the Kingdom.

EPILOG I:

Gnostic Themes in *The Song of the Pearl*

This poem is my adaptation of a 5th century Gnostic text, known as the *Hymn or Song of the Pearl*. My reading of the poem is recorded with accompanying music on the CD *Spirit Soundings*, which consists of spoken word poetry by me with musical accompaniment by Kit Walker and others.

The text I used for my adaptation was published in *The Other Bible*, Edited by Willis Barnstone (Harper & Row, San Francisco, 1984). The editor comments:

> Although the tale was probably pre-Gnostic and pre-Christian, in its present form it has been furnished with details that clearly make it Manichaean…and the young prince and savior is clearly depicted as Mani himself…The hymn exists in an early Syriac text and a somewhat later Greek version. It is attached to the Apocryphal *Acts of Thomas*, which deal with the deeds of the Apostle Judas Thomas.

> For the Gnostics, who tend to reverse Judeo-Christian values, ignorance is equivalent to Judeo-Christian sin and evil. *Gnosis*, brought about through eating the apple from the Tree of Gnosis, (which Christians speak of as original sin) is good and brings redemption. Thus the food that the Prince carries with him is his *gnosis*, which the soul needs to find itself and return to its heavenly home.

I find the following themes, emerging out of the pre-Judeo-Christian Gnostic stream of tradition, particularly appealing to modern spiritual seekers who want to connect with deeper and more ancient Western cultural roots.

The Christian Trinitarian teachings, consisting of God the Father, the Son and the Holy Ghost have been core Church dogma since the 4th century CE Council of Nicaea. This doctrine, distinctly and notoriously, relegates the feminine to lesser divine status. In *The Well of Remembrance*, I have written about the humanly and socially toxic consequences of this distorted Trinitarian doctrine over the past 1500 years.

A much older pre-Christian Trinitarian conception of divinity is reflected in many Gnostic texts, including *The Song of the Pearl*. Here the divine trinity consists of *God-Father, Goddess-Mother* and *God-Child*. This is the divine archetypal trinity that is mirrored in every human family.

According to Gnostic teachings each individual human being also mirrors, reflects and embodies this archetypal structure: *Spirit is Mother-Father* and the *Soul is the originally androgynous Child*, sent out into the world. Being conceived and then born, male or female, into a particular human family, each soul then becomes clothed in the body-mind-persona of a particular human being – and is sent forth into the world.

Another key Gnostic theme found in this and other Gnostic texts holds that each human soul is actually a twin soul. One of the twins incarnates into a human body-and-personality-vehicle, the other one stays behind in the heaven-realm and the two re-unite when the earthly twin vehicle "dies." A truncated and distorted version of this Gnostic teaching remains in the New Testament parable of the return of the Prodigal Son.

Interestingly also, some researchers in human embryology now believe that as many as 40% of all natural conceptions actually have a twin structure – one of which recedes and is re-absorbed by the maternal womb tissue, while the other one continues the journey all the way through birth.

It is possible that some children and adults may remember "losing" a twin brother or sister before birth and may spend time as adults restlessly looking for their "twin soul" in a mate – a quest that could seriously hamper their chance of building a productive relationship.

I have written about these themes in my book *The Life Cycle of the Human Soul.*

EPILOG II:

The Road to Language
Prayer, Speech, Poetry and Narrative

- **Sounds**: cries, moans, groans, screams, roars, yells – raw utterances of primal feelings and reactions.

- **Toning:** singing prolonged, open vowel tones, such as AAH, OOH, UUH, AAY, EEE. Coming from the heart center of feeling, expressed through the throat center. Tones differ from sounds and noises acoustically in their phase coherence.

- **Syllables** or **phonemes:** combinations of vowel-tones – expressing power or energy, and consonants – providing form or structure. They are the building blocks of speech, prayer, poetry and language.

- **Bija mantras:** singular seed syllables, such as OM, AUM, RAM, HUM, VAM, TRAM, HRIH. They resonate with particular energy centers. Central to Indian *nada yoga* and *shabda yoga*.

- **Mantras, prayers and invocations:** clusters of seed syllables, words and divine names, "calling" spiritual beings and their qualities. e.g. *Om Mani Padme Hum; Om Namah Shivaya; Kyrie Elieson; Our Father; La Ilaha Illa'llah; Ave Maria; O Great Spirit; Hare Krishna.*

- **Words and names:** clusters of syllables or phonemes, used to signify and refer to objects, persons, actions, concepts, images, relations, etc.

- **Speech:** sequences of words arranged according to the rules of grammar and semantics, with the intention of communication, e.g. statements, observations, questions, commands, requests.

- **Poetry – epic and lyric:** sequences of words arranged according to semantics *and* the emotional resonances of tone and rhythm.

- **Narratives, stories, histories, novels, theories.**

EPILOG III:

A Riddle with Six Answers

If necessity is the mother of invention – who is the father?

In my book *The Six Pathways of Destiny*, I discuss six possible answers to this question about the impulse behind creative invention.

1. Answer of the artist–storyteller or poet: *creative play.* Playing with new possibilities in the chosen medium can lead to unexpected solutions and inventions.

2. Answer of the builder–organizer: *knowledge of matter.* Knowledge of construction and production can lead to the invention of new material life-supporting systems.

3. Answer of the explorer–scientist: *intuitive insight.* Insight into of the nature of reality leads the scientist to invent concepts and models that deepen understanding and perception.

4. Answer of the healer–shaman: *knowledge of medicine.* The healer–shaman uses innate and acquired knowledge of the healing powers of nature to re-balance and support wholeness.

5. Answer of the teacher–historian: *passion for communication.* The historian–teacher seeks to convey his understanding of the world to expand the consciousness of learners and students.

6. Answer of the warrior–guardian: *conflict and struggle.* Heraclitus said: "war is the father of all things." Conflict generates the need to defend against attack and the continuing invention of more effective strategies.

Besides these six, there is a vast array of destiny pathways, known and unknown. New inventions arise from the interaction between the *yin* of need and the *yang* of insight. The possibilities of creative invention are always open-ended and infinite.

www.ingramcontent.com/pod-product-compliance
Lightning Source LLC
Chambersburg PA
CBHW031239120626
46545CB00003B/1187